Mike, *Love, Marin*

Other mini books in this series:

Cat Quotations
Cricket Quotations
Golf Quotations
Horse Quotations
Mother Quotations
Wine Quotations

Cooks Quotations
Friendship Quotations
Happiness Quotations
Love Quotations
Teddy Bear Quotations

Published simultaneously in 1993 by Exley Publications in Great Britain, and Exley Giftbooks in the USA.
Selection and arrangement © Helen Exley 1993.
Reprinted 1994
Third printing 1995
ISBN 1-85015-435-X
Edited by Helen Exley.
Text research by Patricia Hitchcock.
Designed by Pinpoint Design.
Picture research by P.A. Goldberg and J.M. Clift / Image Select, London.
Typeset by Delta, Watford.
Printed by Kossuth Printing House Co. in Hungary.
Exley Publications Ltd, 16 Chalk Hill, Watford, Herts WD1 4BN, United Kingdom.
Exley Giftbooks, 232 Madison Avenue, Suite 1206, NY 10016, USA.

Acknowledgements: Jilly Cooper: extract from *Mongrel Magic,* published by Mandarin, an imprint of William Heinemann Ltd; Celia Haddon: extracts from *Faithful to the End,* © Celia Haddon 1991, published by Headline Book Publishing plc; Martin Lewis: extracts from *Dogs in the News,* published by Little, Brown & Company; Desmond Morris: extracts from *Dogwatching,* published by Jonathan Cape, 1991; Robert Service: extract from *The Dog Lover's Literary Companion,* published by Prima Publishing © 1992 by John Richard Stephens; John Richard Stephens: extracts from *Dog Lover's Literary Companion,* published by Prima Publishing © 1992 by John Richard Stephens; Loudon Wainwright: extract from *Another Sort of Love Sory,* appeared originally in *Life* Magazine, © 1971 by Time Warner, Inc.
Picture Credits: Cover: Maria Teresa Meloni; Advertising Archive: pages 23, 28; AKG: pages 49, 52; Chris Beetles: pages 16, 54/55; Bonhams, London: pages 21, 41, 42; Bridgeman Art Library: title page and page 8, 18, 21, 31, 32, 34, 37, 41, 43 © Herman Richir, "Detail of the Young Horsewoman", 45 © Arthur Wardle, "Fox Terrier", 47, 56 © Margaret Collyer, "Young boy asleep with dogs", 1905, 58, 61; Cadogan Gallery, London: page 37; Christies, London: page 34; Fine Art Photographic Library Ltd: pages 6, 10, 14, 26, 51; Gavin Graham Gallery, London: page 45; Royal Holloway & Bedford New College: page 18; Imperial Publishing: pages 13, 38; Oscar and Peter Johnson Ltd, London: page 32; Peter Kettle: page 25; John Noott Gallery: page 56; Phillips: page 61; Whitford & Hughes, London: page 58; Christopher Wood Gallery, London: pages 8, 31.

DOG QUOTATIONS

A COLLECTION OF APPEALING PICTURES AND THE BEST DOG QUOTES

EDITED BY
HELEN EXLEY

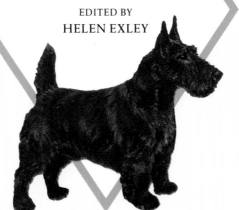

EXLEY
NEW YORK • WATFORD, UK

"Histories are more full of examples of the fidelity of dogs than of friends."

ALEXANDER POPE
in a letter to H. Cromwell, 1709

"There is no faith which has never yet been broken, except that of a truly faithful dog."

KONRAD Z. LORENZ

"Buy a pup and your money will buy love unflinching."

RUDYARD KIPLING

"If there is a heaven, it's certain our animals are to be there. Their lives become so interwoven with our own, it would take more than an archangel to disentangle them."

PAM BROWN, b.1928

THE FIRST FRIEND

"When the Man waked up he said,
'What is Wild Dog doing here?'
And the Woman said,
'His name is not Wild Dog any more,
but the First Friend,
because he will be our friend
for always and always and always.'"

RUDYARD KIPLING

"We have not to gain his confidence or his
friendship: he is born our friend; while
his eyes are still closed, already he believes
in us: even before his birth, he has given
himself to man."

MAURICE MAETERLINCK
from *"My Dog"*

OUR PROTECTORS

"Dogs, bless them, operate on the premise
that human beings are fragile and require
incessant applications of affection and
reassurance. The random lick of the hand and
the furry chin draped over the instep are
calculated to let the shaky owner know that a
friend is nearby."

MARY MCGRORY

Lord, I keep watch!
If I am not here who will guard their house
watch over their sheep? be faithful?
No one but You and I understand
what faithfulness is.
They call me, "Good dog! Nice dog!"
Words....

ANONYMOUS
from *"The Prayer of the Dog"*

—◆—

MAKING PEOPLE HAPPY

"People have a hard time achieving happiness
in their lives. They tend to get wrapped up in
their own little world. People get confused
because they do not know what they need or
want, and then depression sets in. Dogs do
not have this problem. They know exactly
what makes them happy - doing something
for someone. They will do everything they
can think of to please their human
companion, and any signs that they have
been successful make them very happy."

JOHN RICHARD STEPHENS

"Whatever is, is good" - your gracious creed.
You wear your joy of living like a crown.

DOROTHY PARKER

"The dog is a saint. He is straightforward and honest by nature. He knows by instinct when he is not wanted; lies quite still for hours when his king is hard at work. But when his king is sad and worried he creeps up and lays his head on his lap. 'Don't worry. Never mind if they all abandon you. Let us go for a walk and forget all about it!'"

AXEL MUNTHE

— ◆ —

ALMOST HUMAN

"Most dogs don't think they are human; they
know they are."

JANE SWAN

— ◆ —

"To call him a dog hardly seems to do him
justice, though inasmuch as he had four legs,
a tail and barked, I admit he was, to all
outward appearances. But to those of us who
knew him well, he was a perfect gentleman."

HERMIONE GINGOLD (1897-1987)

— ◆ —

"Humankind is drawn to dogs because they
are so like ourselves - bumbling, affectionate,
confused, easily disappointed, eager
to be amused, grateful for kindness and
the least attention."

PAM BROWN, b.1928

— ◆ —

A WELCOME HOME

'Tis sweet to hear the watch-dog's honest bark
Bay deep-mouth'd welcome as we draw near home;
'Tis sweet to know there is an eye will mark
Our coming, and look brighter when we come.

LORD BYRON (1788-1824)
from *"Don Juan"*

— ♦ —

"You come home. The dog throws
itself at you.
'Where have you *been*? You've been so *long*.
I missed you, missed you, missed you. I love
you, love you, love you. What's in the bag?
Something for me? Oh, let me lick your ear.
Oh, let me chew your gloves. You're *Home!*'"

PAM BROWN, b.1928

"The doors swing open - and her face lights
up in incredulous joy. 'You're a silly dog,
then. *Aren't* you a silly dog? I *told* you I
wouldn't be long.' This to a squirm of back, a
flash of paws, a lashing of tail, a bucketing
rump, a leap and a wriggle and a lolling
tongue. The world has come right again."

PAM BROWN, b.1928

SYMPATHETIC NUZZLES

"A loveable St. Bernard named Sherry produced the animal world's answer to all those kissograms delivered by scantily clad girls. She went into business in 1984 with the 'nuzzlegram' - a huge, hairy cuddle complete with a warm, slurpy kiss and an affectionate rub from her cold, wet nose."

MARTYN LEWIS
from *"Dogs In The News"*

— ◆ —

"I, who had had my heart full for hours, took advantage of an early moment of solitude, to cry in it very bitterly. Suddenly a little hairy head thrust itself from behind my pillow into my face, rubbing its ears and nose against me in a responsive agitation, and drying the tears as they came."

ELIZABETH BARRETT BROWNING

— ◆ —

DOGS' EYES

"Far more than by his bark a dog communicates through his eyes – from a soulful half-raised eyebrow when denied a special treat to the wide and sparkling 'Yippee! We're going for a walk!'. Perhaps nothing can wrench the heart of a dog lover more than the pitiful, hardly-daring-to-be-hopeful gaze of an abandoned dog waiting to be adopted."

J.R.E.

— ◆ —

"It is by muteness that a dog becomes for one so utterly beyond value; with him one is at peace, where words play no torturing tricks...Those are the moments that I think are precious to a dog - when, with his adoring soul coming through his eyes, he feels that you are really thinking of him."

JOHN GALSWORTHY

"One of the saddest sights is to see a Dane ill. Their big eyes are a picture of misery, for make no mistake, a sick Dane puts on everything it can to get all the love and sympathy when it feels ill."

BARBARA WOODHOUSE (1910-1988)

— ♦ —

If a dog's prayers were answered, bones would
fall from the sky

PROVERB

— ♦ —

"One rattle of the biscuit tin and you've got
friends for life.
They sit and stare with solemn eyes, and if
you don't take the hint, you get barked at."

JANINE CHUBB, age 10

— ♦ —

"A well-trained dog will make no attempt to
share your lunch. He will just make you feel
so guilty that you cannot enjoy it."

HELEN THOMSON

— ♦ —

"A dog desires affection more than its dinner.
Well - almost."

CHARLOTTE GRAY

THE SATURDAY EVENING

POST

SEPTEMBER 20, 1947   10¢

MISSION: MURDER

EYEWITNESS REPORT OF A
COMMUNIST NIGHT PATROL
IN CHINA
By Jack Belden

BABE DIDRIKSON
TAKES OFF HER MASK
By Pete Martin

WHO IS THE BOSS?

"Most dog owners are at length able to teach
themselves to obey their dog."

ROBERT MORLEY, b. 1908

"He would sit there staring at you; brown and
fat and smelly; slobbering, and sometimes
giving a heavy sigh; and however long a walk
you had taken him, he made you feel that it
ought to have been longer; and however many
biscuits he had had, he made you feel that he
ought to have had more. Frances tells me that
there was a legend in her family that Sancho
was nearly always kept chained up; this was
entirely untrue, but it just shows the force of
his character that he was able to impose this
idea on them from a distance."

GWEN RAVERAT

No Bob! I will not go a walk -
I am not feeling very fit:
I'd much prefer to sit and talk,
Or sit and read, - or simply sit.

··●●··

It's very hot: there's lots of dust -
I really do not think I can....
Well, if you look like that, I must -
Are you my Dog? No, I'm your Man.

ROBERT BELL

— ◆ —

NUISANCES!

"A door is what a dog is perpetually on the wrong side of."

OGDEN NASH
from *"A Dog's Best Friend Is His Illiteracy"*, 1953

"The most affectionate creature in the world is a wet dog."

AMBROSE BIERCE (1842-1914)

"Montmorency [the dog] came and sat on things just when they were wanted to be packed. He put his leg into the jam, and he worried the teaspoons, and he pretended that the lemons were rats, and got into the hamper and killed three of them."

JEROME K. JEROME
from *"Three Men In A Boat"*

"Every puppy should have a boy."

ERMA BOMBECK, b.1927

— ◆ —

"The dog was created especially for children.
He is the god of frolic."

HENRY WARD BEECHER.

— ◆ —

"The dog hesitated for a moment, but
presently made some little advances with his
tail. The child put out his hand and called
him. In an apologetic manner the dog came
close, and the two had an interchange of
friendly pattings and waggles."

STEPHEN CRANE

— ◆ —

"I love my dog because it is the closest thing I
have. And ... it may give you the soft look."

KEVIN JONES, age 14

— ◆ —

LAZYBONES

"He toils not, neither does he spin, yet Solomon in all his glory never lay upon a door-mat all day long, sun-soaked and fly-fed and fat, while his master worked for the means wherewith to purchase an idle wag of Solomonic tail, seasoned with a look of tolerant recognition."

AMBROSE BIERCE (1842-1914)

— ♦ —

I like the way that the world is made,
(Tickle me, please, behind the ears)
With part in the sun and part in the shade
(Tickle me, please, behind the ears).
This comfortable spot beneath a tree
Was probably planned for you and me;
Why do you suppose God made a flea?
Tickle me more behind the ears.

BURGES JOHNSON

— ♦ —

"He leads a dog's life," people cry -
But why?...
All day you do exactly as you feel;
You sleep before, and after, every meal.
Things would be said
If I had so much bed!

A. P. HERBERT

"The more I see of men, the more I like dogs."

MADAME DE STAEL

"The dog has seldom
been successful in pulling man
up to its level of sagacity, but man has
frequently dragged the dog down to his."

JAMES THURBER

— ◆ —

"If you pick up a starving dog and make him
prosperous, he will not bite you. This is the
principal difference between a dog and man."

MARK TWAIN

— ◆ —

"Maybe there are some areas where, when we
are compared to dogs, we come up short.
Being called a 'dog' might not be such a bad
thing after all."

JOHN RICHARD STEPHENS

GIVING THEIR LIVES

"Excavators digging through the volcanic ash that buried the ruins of Pompeii in A.D. 79 discovered a dog lying across a child. The dog, whose name was Delta, wore a collar that told how he had saved the life of his owner, Severinus, three times."

JOHN RICHARD STEPHENS

"The plain fact that my dog loves me more than I love him is undeniable and always fills me with a certain feeling of shame. The dog is ever ready to lay down his life for me."

KONRAD Z. LORENZ

ALL SHAPES AND SIZES

"The uglier the dog, the more he or she is loved."

MARTYN LEWIS

"He is so shaggy. People are amazed when he gets up and they suddenly realize they have been talking to the wrong end."

ELIZABETH JONES

"A dog is a smile and a wagging tail. What is in between doesn't matter much."

CLARA ORTEGA

"Dachshunds are ideal dogs for small children, as they are already stretched and pulled to such a length that the child cannot do much harm one way or the other."

ROBERT BENCHLEY (1889-1945)

ABANDONED AND LOST

"A lost dog is a sad sight. They have a particular, desperate gait, a confused urgency, eyes too anxious to respond to any call. They move fast through unknown territory, hoping against hope to hear a familiar voice, scent familiar ground - and all the while moving deeper and deeper into desolation."

PAM BROWN, b.1928

— ◆ —

"Visiting a dogs' home is a gruelling experience - all those desperate creatures clamouring for attention. For the tender-hearted it is not hard to come away with a whole pack."

JILLY COOPER
from *"Mongrel Magic"*

"To a man the greatest blessing is individual liberty, to a dog is the last word in despair."

WILLIAM LYON PHELPS

"'Won't be long' means nothing to a dog. All he knows is that you are GONE."

JANE SWAN

Oh, the saddest of sights in a world of sin
Is a little lost pup with his tail tucked in!

ARTHUR GUITERMAN

SMELLS, GLORIOUS SMELLS!

"A human walk in the twilight is a pallid affair
to that being experienced by their dog.
Rabbit. Mouse. The dog at the house next
door. The ginger tom. Toffee. Dead bird.
Earthworm. Pizza wrappings. The dog from
number seven. Unknown cat. Frog."

PAM BROWN, b.1928

"Examples of this sweat-detection ability are
amazingly impressive....Bloodhounds can
follow a trail that is as much as four days old
and track a subject for up to a hundred miles.
The scent from human feet is so strong to a dog
that it can identify individual feet even in areas
where many other feet have trodden, and
where shoes have been worn by all concerned."

DESMOND MORRIS
from *"Dogwatching"*

— ◆ —

"When did any dog turn up his nose at a smell....Times are, indeed, when smelliness pure and simple, quantity rather than quality, just the ineffable affluence of Nature's bounty to the nose, seems to ravish one of these great lovers almost clean off the earth."

C. E. MONTAGUE

"A dog believes you are what you think you are."

JANE SWAN

— ♦ —

"You've seen that look. The way a young painter looks at a Rembrandt or Titian. The way Liz Taylor looks at Richard Burton. The way Zsa Zsa looks at mink. That's how a poodle looks at its master."

JACQUELINE SUSANN (1921-1974)

— ♦ —

"Our dogs will love and admire the meanest of us, and feed our colossal vanity with their uncritical homage."

AGNES REPPLIER

— ♦ —

"No one appreciates the very special genius of your conversation as a dog does."

CHRISTOPHER MORLEY

"Montmorency's ambition in life is to get in the way and be sworn at. If he can squirm in anywhere where he particularly is not wanted...he feels his day has not been wasted."

JEROME K. JEROME

"...this one wasn't perfect. Now and then his taste in food would turn to garbage and he upset many cans in search for the ripest morsels. He dug holes in lawns and he liked to sprawl on young plants. He was a discoverer of mud. When he found something - often invisible and even nonexistent - to bark at, he barked hard and he ignored commands to stop and come the hell home."

LOUDON WAINWRIGHT

TIME FOR A WALK...

"A score of times I have told him that he had much better not come; I have announced fiercely that he is not to come. He then lets go of his legs...and, laying his head between his front paws, stares at me through the red haws that make his eyes so mournful. He will do this for an hour without blinking, for he knows that in time it will unman me. My dog knows very little, but what little he does know he knows extraordinarily well. One can get out of my chambers by a back way, and I sometimes steal softly - but I can't help looking back, and there he is, and there are those haws asking sorrowfully, 'Is this worthy of you?' 'Curse you,' I say, 'get your hat,' or words to that effect..."

J. M. BARRIE

— ◆ —

"Of course what he most intensely dreams of is being taken out on walks, and the more you are able to indulge him the more will he adore you and the more all the latent beauty of his nature will come out."

HENRY JAMES
on his dog Max

NO QUESTIONS ASKED

"He is very imprudent, a dog is. He never makes it his business to inquire whether you are in the right or in the wrong, never bothers as to whether you are going up or down upon life's ladder, never asks whether you are rich or poor, silly or wise, sinner or saint. Come luck or misfortune, good repute or bad, honour or shame, he is going to stick to you, to comfort you, guard you, and give his life for you...."

JEROME K. JEROME

"Pug is come! - come to fill up the void left by false and narrow-hearted friends. I see already that he is without envy, hatred, or malice - that he will betray no secrets, and feel neither pain at my success nor pleasure in my chagrin."

GEORGE ELIOT (MARY ANN EVANS)

HELPERS

"...people who keep dogs (or cats, for that matter) live longer on average than those who do not. This is not some kind of pro-canine campaigning fantasy. It is a simple medical fact that the calming influence of the company of a friendly pet animal reduces blood pressure and therefore the risk of heart attack."

DESMOND MORRIS

"Guide dogs for the blind, hearing dogs for the deaf, dog companions for those that live alone.... Dogs who comfort the sick and the elderly and befriend lonely children. All over the world there are hundreds of thousands of these faithful animals serving us with their love."

J.R.E.

FOR THE LONELY

"I have found that when you are deeply troubled there are things you get from the silent devoted companionship of a dog that you can get from no other source."

DORIS DAY, b.1924

"...the first, the earliest delight, is derived from physical contact. And physical contact it is that makes a pet animal so precious to lonely people."

DILYS POWELL
from *"Animals in My Life"*

"Puppies are nature's remedy for feeling unloved...plus numerous other ailments of life."

RICHARD ALLAN PALM

"A few creatures fear us, most are unaware of us and not one loves us...Now in this indifference...in this incommunicable world...where exist among created things no other relations than those of executioners and victims, eaters and eaten...one animal alone, among all that breathes upon the earth, has succeeded in breaking through the prophetic circle, in escaping from itself to come bounding towards us...This animal, our good familiar dog,... has nevertheless performed one of the most unusual and improbable acts that we can find in the general history of life..."

MAURICE MAETERLINCK
from "My Dog"

"A loving friendship, formed over thousands of years, flourishes between dogs and human beings. Dogs have left the hunting pack of their ancestors and have become members of our human world."

CELIA HADDON

"We are alone, absolutely alone on this chance planet: and, amid all the forms of life that surround us, not one, excepting the dog has made an alliance with us."

MAURICE MAETERLINCK

FAITHFUL FOREVER

"He will sleep on the cold ground where the wintry winds blow and the snow drives fiercely if only he may be near his master's side. He will kiss the hand that has no food to offer. He will lick the wounds and sores that come in encounter with the roughness of the

world. He guards the sleep of his pauper master as if he were a prince."

SENATOR GEORGE G. VEST

— ◆ —

"The time comes to every dog when it ceases to care for people merely for biscuits or bones, or even for caresses, and walks out of doors. When a dog *really* loves, it prefers the person who gives it nothing, and perhaps is too ill ever to take it out for exercise...."

FRANCES P. COBBE (1822-1904)

— ◆ —

"The man was stretched on the pavement brutishly drunk and dead to the world. The dog, lying by his side, seemed to look at me with sad, imploring eyes. Though all the world despised that man, I thought, this poor brute loves him and will be faithful to death."

ROBERT SERVICE
from *"Ballads of a Bohemian"*

<u>"PLEASE LOVE ME"</u>

"Inside every Newfoundland, Boxer,
Elkhound and Great Dane is a puppy longing
to climb on to your lap."

HELEN THOMSON, b.1943

"If I sit down on a bench he is at my side at
once and takes up a position on one of my
feet. For it is a law of his being that he only
runs about when I am in motion too; that
when I settle down he follows suit."

THOMAS MANN
from *"A Man and His Dog"*

"The average dog has one request to all
humankind.
Love me."

HELEN EXLEY

<u>ABSOLUTE LOVE</u>

"A dog has one aim in life. To bestow his heart."

J. R. ACKERLEY

"A dog is the only thing on this earth that loves you more than he loves himself."

JOSH BILLINGS (HENRY WHEELER SHAW) (1818-1885)

Sign on bulletin board: "Puppies for sale: The only love that money can buy."

"Dogs are indeed the most social, affectionate, and amiable animals of the whole brute creation..."

EDMUND BURKE